D1169861

IT'S TIME TO TAKE BACK OUR COUNTRY

Kevin L. Zadai

IT'S TIME TO TAKE BACK OUR COUNTRY

IT'S TIME TO TAKE BACK OUR COUNTRY

IT'S TIME TO TAKE BACK OUR COUNTRY

Cover design by: Virtually Possible Designs

For more information about our school, go to Warriornotesschool.com.

Reach us on the Internet: Kevinzadai.com

ISBN 13 TP: 9798696406480

For Worldwide Distribution, Printed in the U.S.A.

INTRODUCTION

""Assuredly, I say to you, whatever you bind on Earth will be bound in heaven, and whatever you loose on Earth will be loosed in heaven. "Again I say to you that if two of you agree on earth concerning anything that they ask, it will be done for them by My Father in heaven." Matthew 18:18-19

The Spirit of God is desiring that we permit Him to help us to pray out the will of God for our lives. The proper time to pray is "always" according to the apostle Paul. In Ephesians 6:18 he says, "Praying always with all prayer and supplication in the Spirit, being watchful to this end with all perseverance and supplication for all the saints"

Recently, while in a dream-state, I had a powerful visitation that lasted all night where Jesus gave me the most compelling revelations. He showed me what was

IT'S TIME TO TAKE BACK OUR COUNTRY

occurring in the spiritual realm all around us. Jesus also showed me the future and how to pray specifically for the people of our country. This prayer book, "It's Time To Take Back Our Country" is a result of this visitation.

Please pray continually using these prayer points to secure our nation for years to come as we see the largest, most abundant harvest of souls we have ever seen in a generation.

Pray Fervently!

Kevin Zadai
Founder and President of Warrior Notes Ministries

PRAYER POINT

1

LUKEWARMNESS

"I know your works, that you are neither cold nor hot. I could wish you were cold or hot. So then, because you are lukewarm, and neither cold nor hot, I will vomit you out of My mouth." (Revelation 3:15-16)

One of the things that Jesus spent a lot of time with me about in the five-hour visitation I had in May of 2020, was lukewarmness, and how believers do not understand their authority. They do not understand who they are in Christ, and they seem to back off and to live in a compromised position. I often find that unless someone or something happens to show people that they have backed off and have compromised, they don't realize how lukewarm they have become.

IT'S TIME TO TAKE BACK OUR COUNTRY

In the Old Testament we read about the prophet Jeremiah who was a plumb line to Israel. Jesus showed me that this is what prophets are supposed to do. They are supposed to be plumb lines. They are supposed to inform people of what God is saying, which might be a standard that is way higher than what we are currently experiencing. So, because of that, Jesus talked to me a lot about lukewarmness, so I want to reiterate this.

For this very first prayer point, I want to emphasize that we need to pray against lukewarmness, *because there are no history makers that are lukewarm!* They are red hot for the Lord.

Lukewarmness must go from a believer's life. And when it goes from the believer's life, it will go from the church's life. The church is not really the church unless you have the body, the people. We need to have a group of on-fire people that stand together in unity. One of us on our own is not the entire body of Christ. We are part of the body, so we need everyone to come together.

I am emphasizing to you that Lukewarmness must leave the believer's life. We must get the holy fire from the altar of God, and we must stand up for what is right and that will take us to a higher temperature rating. The same temperature as the flames that are on the altar of God right now! The angels that are there at the altar are burning with holy fire. The angels that come to you at night to talk to you, to give you dreams and burning with fire. The angels that are with you during the day, they are flames of fire.

"And of the angels He says: '"Who makes His angels spirits and His ministers a flame of fire."' Hebrews 1:7

"Are they not all ministering spirits sent forth to minister for those who will inherit salvation?" Hebrews 1:14

Angels are ministering spirits sent to minister for those who are going to inherit salvation. The book of Hebrews clearly shows us that these angels are sent by God and that they are flames of fire, sent on special assignments.

"For He shall give His angels charge over you, to keep you in all your ways." Psalm 91:11

Angels are assigned special assignments to keep us in all our ways. Always remember that angels are hot with the fire of God! The fire of God from the altar is hot so we need to be hot. We need to get rid of anything in our lives that prevent us from being as hot as we could be.

When we get hot, the body of Christ gets hot, the church is hot. Then we have a manifestation of God on the earth, through the church, and we will see a change in our nation!

We need to ask forgiveness for our lukewarmness, and anything that we've done in our lives that has prevented us from being hot. We need to repent and get right with God; let's just get on with it. Let all sin and neglect be taken care of, and let's just become really good soldiers of Christ!

Prayer

Father, I pray that every person reading this, that you would douse them with the fire from heaven and that you baptize them with fire. Baptize them with holy fire right now in the name of Jesus.

We pray for our nation. We pray that every believer on the soil in the United States and other countries around the world, that we would be doused with holy fire and that we would not be lukewarm, and that the body of Christ would rise up in their authority and who they are. That we would walk in what Jesus has accomplished by being seated with Him, in the heavenly realms and that we would recognize that we are far above all ruling authority through Jesus Christ.

And we take authority and break the powers of the devil and we say, Lord, that we're not going to be lukewarm. We are going to be counted as hot in this day, Lord. We are going to be the temperature that you have preordained for us, Lord. And I thank you for it in the name of Jesus.

IT'S TIME TO TAKE BACK OUR COUNTRY

What did the Holy Spirit reveal to you regarding this prayer point?

_____

_____

_____

_____

_____

_____

_____

_____

_____

_____

_____

_____

_____

_____

_____

_____

_____

_____

_____

_____

_____

_____

_____

_____

IT'S TIME TO TAKE BACK OUR COUNTRY

PRAYER POINT

2

Serving Others

"Let love be without hypocrisy. Abhor what is evil. Cling to what is good. Be kindly affectionate to one another with brotherly love, in honor giving preference to one another; not lagging in diligence, fervent in spirit, serving the Lord; rejoicing in hope, patient in tribulation, continuing steadfastly in prayer; distributing to the needs of the saints, given to hospitality." (Romans 12:9-13)

The next prayer point I want to share with you is about serving others in this time that we are living in. You have to remember that satan wants everyone to hole up and be alone and to be in a survival mode. It is actually a false doctrine to be holed up right now. You have to know what the Spirit of the Lord is saying in this hour.

IT'S TIME TO TAKE BACK OUR COUNTRY

This is the time to be out there preaching the Good News and telling people that the Lord Jesus Christ and Father God are good. God is a good God! They are not doing these terrible things that are coming upon the Earth. It happens because we are in a fallen world that is under a curse. But the good news is that each one of us can reconcile people to God. We have a ministry of reconciliation whereby we go out and proclaim that people's sins have been forgiven and that the price has been paid and that God is not angry anymore because of the great sacrifice of Jesus.

"Therefore, if anyone is in Christ, he is a new creation; old things have passed away; behold, all things have become new. Now all things are of God, who has reconciled us to Himself through Jesus Christ, and has given us the ministry of reconciliation, that is, that God was in Christ reconciling the world to Himself, not imputing their trespasses to them, and has committed to us the word of reconciliation." 2 Corinthians 5:17-19

Just tell people to repent of their sins, accept Jesus as the only way to the Heavenly Father, and they will be saved. Right now, we need to be telling people this. This is your ministry from Heaven. This is how each one of you can serve others. Tell people that the devil is the one that's doing these terrible things in the world and that it's not God.

IT'S TIME TO TAKE BACK OUR COUNTRY

Jesus wants you to preach the Gospel. Jesus told me, "Kevin, don't back off. Serve others. Do things for others." So, when you go to the grocery store, get something for someone else, buy two of something. You buy one for yourself, and you buy one for someone else. God gave us a heart to love and to serve people, and that is what we are supposed to be doing. We are not supposed to be holed up, waiting for the antichrist to come because he is not coming any time soon. He is not coming until Jesus removes the one who is holding him back. That is us. We are still here, and we are holding the Antichrist back. We are ruining the devil's party! Every single day that you wake up, you are ruining the devil's party because he cannot do a thing on your watch because you are a good watchman. So, we pray. We pray against those evil spirits that would want to get people into a survival mode through fear. We pray against fear. Jesus is asking that you would serve people and go forth in the love of God.

Everywhere you go, tell people that God is a loving God and that He cares about people; He wants them to come to the knowledge of Lord Jesus Christ. He wants us to tell people about Him. And if you will do this, you will prophesy and testify of Jesus. You are going to see miracles. You are going to see signs and wonders. We are seeing people healed during our global prayer meetings that we are having online. We have so many reports of people getting healed during our prayer meetings. God is a good God!

IT'S TIME TO TAKE BACK OUR COUNTRY

Serve others! Be mindful of all the people around you and sense their needs. Be a giver.

PRAYER

Father, thank you that we are not given a spirit of fear, but of love and of power and of a sound mind. I thank you, Lord. We pray that in this nation, all the believers stand up and become bold to speak their faith and that they are given over to a giving heart, Father and that they would allow You to use them to give to others.

And even in their time of need, Lord, we pray that your people will buy extra to give and serve others. Father, we just want to show Your love to people. We break that spirit of fear right now and any kind of spirit that's causing people to hole up and back off and to hide, in the name of Jesus. I pray for boldness right now. I pray for boldness for every believer that we would stand up in our authority in the name of Jesus.

IT'S TIME TO TAKE BACK OUR COUNTRY

What did the Holy Spirit reveal to you regarding this prayer point?

_____
_____
_____
_____
_____
_____
_____
_____
_____
_____
_____
_____
_____
_____
_____
_____
_____
_____
_____
_____
_____
_____
_____

IT'S TIME TO TAKE BACK OUR COUNTRY

PRAYER POINT

3

<u>Wisdom and Understanding</u>

"that the God of our Lord Jesus Christ, the Father of glory, may give to you the spirit of wisdom and revelation in the knowledge of Him, the eyes of your understanding being enlightened; that you may know what is the hope of His calling, what are the riches of the glory of His inheritance in the saints, and what is the exceeding greatness of His power toward us who believe, according to the working of His mighty power." (Ephesians 1:17-19)

The Lord wants us to pray for wisdom and understanding in all our ways because His ways should be our ways. We do not know His ways as we should. He said that His ways are higher than our ways, but we can come to know His ways; we *can* know the mind of Christ.

IT'S TIME TO TAKE BACK OUR COUNTRY

"For 'who has known the mind of the LORD that he may instruct Him?' But we have the mind of Christ." 1 Corinthians 2:16

If we know the mind of Christ, how should we be praying? As you read in the verses at the beginning of this chapter, Paul told the Ephesians in chapter one, to pray that the spirit of wisdom and revelation in the knowledge of Him would be upon us. We are to pray that our inner man would be lit up with wisdom and understanding from the other realm. This is the way that Paul prayed. He said that we can understand our inheritance and what it is that God has done for us through Jesus Christ. We have the understanding, as well as the power of the resurrection.

We do have eyes to see. We do have ears to hear. We know the hope to which we have been called. We know the glorious inheritance in the saints. And we also know the power that rose Jesus from the dead.

Jesus wanted me to tell people that they need to begin praying this prayer in Ephesians. Put your own name in this powerful prayer that Paul prayed. I do not pray for myself often, but when I do, this is one that I pray.

We need to understand the greatness and the power that has been given to us— that is within us. If we understood this, we would not be backing off right now. We would say, "You know what? I want to see things changed and I am going to call the shots!" You begin to call for righteousness and justice to come back into our system and our government; you begin to proclaim the Lord's favor on believers.

You see, right now, we are in Goshen. In other words, we are in the land that the Israelites dwelt while in slavery. They did not receive any of those terrible plagues like Egypt did. They were eventually delivered out of it and they received their promised land. And that was a type and shadow of what we are encountering right now. We are in Goshen. We are in the secret place, and we are partaking of God's blessing and favor.

We will not be judged during this time. We will not encounter the things that the world will encounter because God does not judge His children with the world. We are to stand out from among the world and then we are not judged. This is why it is called the Gospel; it's good news!

PRAYER

I pray, Father, right now, in the name of Jesus, for every believer all over the world, I pray that they have eyes to see and ears to hear and that their spirit would be enlightened with Your spirit, with knowledge and wisdom, and with revelation.

IT'S TIME TO TAKE BACK OUR COUNTRY

And I know, Lord God, that You want to show them the inheritance that they have and how good You are. I know that You want to show them how much You love them. And I know that You want to show them and have them understand the power that rose Jesus from the dead. Father, I thank You right now that by Your Spirit, You are touching everyone. We pray for every believer on the Earth right now, Lord, that they would rise up and that even our president and all of our leaders would have a spirit of wisdom and revelation and that their eyes would be open.

We do not want any of those people to go to hell. And I thank you, Father, that they would repent right now and turn from their wicked ways and that they would live an upright life. I pray, Lord God because no one is too hard of a case, for You. I just ask for repentance among Congress and repentance among our leadership in the name of Jesus. I thank You for our justice system; I pray that all of the unjust judges would repent of their sins right now and that they would turn to God. Give them one last chance before they go to hell.

I call out to every judge, every senator, every congressman, and every representative. I call you to repentance right now. Just repent of your sins and represent righteousness and justice in this country in the name of Jesus. Amen!

IT'S TIME TO TAKE BACK OUR COUNTRY

What did the Holy Spirit reveal to you regarding this prayer point?

_____

_____

_____

_____

_____

_____

_____

_____

_____

_____

_____

_____

_____

_____

_____

_____

_____

_____

_____

_____

_____

_____

_____

_____

IT'S TIME TO TAKE BACK OUR COUNTRY

PRAYER POINT

4

<u>Words Anointed With Fire</u>

"Then one of the seraphim flew to me, having in his hand a live coal which he had taken with the tongs from the altar. And he touched my mouth with it, and said: 'Behold, this has touched your lips; Your iniquity is taken away, and your sin purged.' Also I heard the voice of the Lord, saying: 'Whom shall I send, and who will go for Us?' Then I said, 'Here am I! Send me.' (Isaiah 6:6-8)

Another prayer point that the Lord gave me was that our words have to be anointed with fire. Are your words being spoken from the fire?

There is a proximity that comes where you get closer and closer to the Father and then you start acting like Him. It's when I find that my will becomes His will. When I am

IT'S TIME TO TAKE BACK OUR COUNTRY

in His presence and understand that His ways are so much higher than mine, I can get overwhelmed. Sometimes I almost sense what it's like to be in Heaven again and feel that authority and His awesome power. God does not sit there and worry about anything. He is so gracious with us right now that He doesn't judge us according to our sins. He judges us according to what the blood is speaking—the blood of Jesus.

When we speak, we should be speaking anointed words of fire. We speak from the fire regarding the direction we are going, where our country is going. We speak that the judges are going to make just judgments and that our Congress will represent the people and not themselves. We speak that the Attorney General will go through with all the indictments that he has, in the name of Jesus, and that he will use the authority that is vested in him as the Attorney General. So, all believers everywhere should be speaking these anointed words of fire. We speak that the Attorney General succeeds in his mission. That the President succeeds in his mission. That Congress succeeds in the mission that is in God's heart for this country, and that they represent righteousness, justice, and truth.

This is how we speak. We speak from the fire. Now, this seems crazy to some people, but see, God is not normal. He is not normal in the way that we know normal. God is way above, far above, but when you get close to Him, you will start acting like Him.

IT'S TIME TO TAKE BACK OUR COUNTRY

"Therefore be imitators of God as dear children" Ephesians 5:1

We are supposed to imitate God. So, what is He doing right now? Well, He's laughing at his enemies.

"He who sits in the heavens shall laugh; The Lord shall hold them in derision." Psalm 2:4

He laughs that His enemies are coming to nothing. It says that He sits in Heaven, and He knows that His enemies are coming to nothing. Why? Because Jesus made a show of the enemy openly, not even in secret.

"Having disarmed principalities and powers, He made a public spectacle of them, triumphing over them in it." Colossians 2:15

And it says it says in 1 John that He came to destroy the works of the devil!

"He who sins is of the devil, for the devil has sinned from the beginning. For this purpose the Son of God was manifested, that He might destroy the works of the devil." 1 John 3:8

Jesus came to destroy the works of the devil, and so, we should be enforcing that right now! We should be trampling on serpents and scorpions (see Luke 10:19). We should not be screaming and being afraid of them and getting someone else to get rid of the serpents and scorpions. We are supposed to trample on them!

There is no compassion for the enemy. When we lived in Arizona and had scorpions, I wasn't compassionate with them. I would just yell, "die, die." Then I would say, "Look at you now, you're powerless." The scorpions would be limping around because I was trampling them whenever they tried to come in my house. It was the same with the snakes that tried to come into my house! We had all kinds of animals in the desert there where we lived.

Holy fire causes us to proclaim the Word, but the Word is going to be higher than what we may be living under at the moment, but we have to speak where we are going. So, we speak from the fire. You speak where you're going. You speak from the anointing. You break the yoke over your leadership. You command those evil spirits to let go of your leadership.

PRAYER

I command every evil spirit to let go of our leadership that they do the work of Father God. That even if they are just like King Cyrus, they just do the work of God, even if they are not a believing one. God, you can still use them. I just believe, Lord, that You are going to cause peace to come.

And I pray, Father, that believers everywhere would speak from the fire and proclaim where they are going according

IT'S TIME TO TAKE BACK OUR COUNTRY

to the Word of God. They will speak where our nation is going according to the heart of God.

And I thank you, Lord God, that we speak from the fire and that all the believers everywhere across the globe, they will speak from their authority. They speak from the fire in the name of Jesus. Amen.

IT'S TIME TO TAKE BACK OUR COUNTRY

What did the Holy Spirit reveal to you regarding this prayer point?

_____

_____

_____

_____

_____

_____

_____

_____

_____

_____

_____

_____

_____

_____

_____

_____

_____

_____

_____

_____

_____

_____

_____

PRAYER POINT

5

Believe For The Greater Works

"Most assuredly, I say to you, he who believes in Me, the works that I do he will do also; and greater works than these he will do, because I go to My Father." (John 14:12)

Jesus said that we need to believe for the greater works. It's time for us to not just pray for ourselves and for a couple of people we know but for the greater works.

Jesus wants us to take back what the devil stole. There is payback coming! Whatever your suffering is, whether it is back wages or your health, whatever has happened the last few months, it's payback time.

As the devil is on his way out of your life because you have cast him out and have broken his power, say, "Hey, not so fast. You owe me seven times!" You see, you have to go a step further than what you would normally be doing. We have to go after the greater works. It's one thing to cast the devil out. I mean, it's amazing when you cast him out, but then there are the greater works.

I heard about a minister that was sitting in a room where the devil moved the bed in front of them. So, he told the devil to leave, but then the minister said to the devil, "You know what, before you leave, move the bed back!" And he made the devil move it back! This is just one example of the greater works. You need to believe in the greater works as you seek God's face.

We know that the greater works are going to come through us. It's not going to be us doing them, but it's going to be our Father doing it through us. We must step it up. It's not just enough for the enemy to be caught, he has to repay. For instance, don't just believe for your own healing, but while you're at it, believe for your whole family's healing! Just take it by force. This is another example of the greater works you are going to do. Don't allow anything to make you back off of this!

PRAYER

Father, I pray that we will not only see your works, not only will we see the works of Jesus, not only will we see the works of the Holy Spirit, but we will see the greater works. I pray that the power of your Holy Spirit goes out right now

IT'S TIME TO TAKE BACK OUR COUNTRY

to everyone that is reading this, and they will receive this impartation

Jesus, you want us to move into the greater works. And this means that the whole body of Christ must come into unity and become mature and start to see the Father's heart come through and that the enemy must pay back sevenfold in the name of Jesus. Thank you, Father.

IT'S TIME TO TAKE BACK OUR COUNTRY

What did the Holy Spirit reveal to you regarding this prayer point?

_____

_____

_____

_____

_____

_____

_____

_____

_____

_____

_____

_____

_____

_____

_____

_____

_____

_____

_____

_____

_____

_____

_____

_____

PRAYER POINT

6

Vote In Heaven—Vote On Earth

"'Assuredly, I say to you, whatever you bind on Earth will be bound in heaven, and whatever you loose on Earth will be loosed in heaven. 'Again I say to you that if two of you agree on earth concerning anything that they ask, it will be done for them by My Father in heaven.'" (Matthew 18:18-19)

Jesus told me that in prayer, we are to go and vote in heaven first and then vote on Earth. We are supposed to go to the throne room and say, "we are not going to have it this way." We can bind, we can loose, and we can agree as touching any one thing, and it will be done for us. In these verses, there is nothing that says, "except in these conditions," nothing that says it might not even happen.

IT'S TIME TO TAKE BACK OUR COUNTRY

"Ask, and it will be given to you; seek, and you will find; knock, and it will be opened to you. For everyone who asks receives, and he who seeks finds, and to him who knocks it will be opened." Matthew 7:7-8

It says if you ask, you are going to receive. If you seek, you are going to find. If you knock, the doors can be opened for you. This is absolute truth that you need to believe for your life. This is the believer's authority. This is the way we operate.

We need to go to Heaven first and vote. That's what Jesus was telling me, that we vote in Heaven. In other words, we pray and forbid the injustice in our nation. We forbid unrighteousness to be in our nation. Then we go to the polls, and we vote the heart of God. We vote people out who are not doing the will of our Father in Heaven and not doing the people's will.

There are many believers in this nation that need to get out and vote, you must vote for righteousness, and for justice. You need to vote for life, not death. You need a vote for the rights of people and not the rights of a government. You need to know that you are not voting for the government, you are voting for people.

When you vote on Earth, you are choosing who is going to represent you; you should choose wisely in that. In any case, you should always choose life. The Lord told me to give voice to the children because the children do not have a voice. Babies do not have a voice. Jesus told me that the church is supposed to be the voice of the children. So, we are saying "no" to abortion. We are saying "no" to sex trafficking. We are saying "no" to all the wickedness that is going on. The children have a right to have a voice. So, we vote in Heaven, and we forbid it. But then we go to the polls, and we enforce that vote.

PRAYER

Father, I pray that everyone has boldness in the name of Jesus. I pray Lord God that everyone will go to Heaven right now into the throne room of God and be seated with Christ as they already are and see the throne and see their authority right now.

Lord, we agree as touching this one thing, that righteousness shall reign, that justice shall reign in our nation. The redeemed of the Lord say so!

Lord, we agree with You on everything, and whoever is in government that does not want to enforce that, they must go in Jesus' name right now. And so, Lord, we pray that the people have the ability and the boldness to go and vote and show up at the polls and vote for righteousness and vote for the life of babies and vote for justice and truth in Jesus' name.

IT'S TIME TO TAKE BACK OUR COUNTRY

What did the Holy Spirit reveal to you regarding this prayer point?

_____

_____

_____

_____

_____

_____

_____

_____

_____

_____

_____

_____

_____

_____

_____

_____

_____

_____

_____

_____

_____

_____

_____

_____

PRAYER POINT

7

Lay The Ax At The Root

"And even now the ax is laid to the root of the trees. Therefore every tree which does not bear good fruit is cut down and thrown into the fire." (Luke 3:9)

Jesus told me that we need to lay the ax at the root, and it will sever the life of the vine, tree, or whatever is growing that is not from the Father. The Lord told me that we need to cut off evil at the root and stop the unrighteousness that we are seeing.

We need to lay the ax at the root of corruption in the government, and in Hollywood, and everywhere else that unrighteousness and injustice are being promoted. There are many people that are being influenced by the enemy to propagate an evil agenda throughout this nation. So, in prayer, we must lay the ax at the root to all the evil that is working behind the scenes in all those places. As we lay the ax at the root and believe that these evil forces are taken down, at the same time, we declare acts of righteousness to come forth in these areas.

The enemy has his agenda, and Father God has His agenda. God will never allow Himself to be put in checkmate. He reserves the last move for Himself, but we have to pray. We have to do our part to see righteousness prevail.

"Therefore I say to you, whatever things you ask when you pray, believe that you receive them, and you will have them." Mark 11:24

PRAYER

Father, in the name of Jesus, we lay the ax at the root of all evil in this country and all over the world. We lay the ax at the root of all acts of unrighteousness, and we sever all the life that these evil spirits are giving and empowering the leadership in this country and all other countries.

We forbid these evil spirits to operate in the name of Jesus. We come against these powers with the blood of Jesus. We put the blood of Jesus on the walls of every believer's heart and the walls of every person's house right now. Lord, we stand up for righteousness, and we ask for protection,

IT'S TIME TO TAKE BACK OUR COUNTRY

Father, and we sever that evil in Hollywood. We sever that satanic evil in our government in Jesus' name.

And we thank you, Lord, that the people that are enforcing these terrible things on this Earth are powerless against You. Lord God, You are the great and mighty God. The Lord's will shall be accomplished because the power that is behind these people is going away.

*The Lord says that these people will just disappear. They will not be able to carry out their plans and purposes, which are evil.

IT'S TIME TO TAKE BACK OUR COUNTRY

What did the Holy Spirit reveal to you regarding this prayer point?

_____

_____

_____

_____

_____

_____

_____

_____

_____

_____

_____

_____

_____

_____

_____

_____

_____

_____

_____

_____

_____

_____

_____

_____

_____

PRAYER POINT

8

Speak The Father's Words

"For I have not spoken on My own authority; but the Father who sent Me gave Me a command, what I should say and what I should speak. And I know that His command is everlasting life. Therefore, whatever I speak, just as the Father has told Me, so I speak.'" (John 12:49-50)

You must speak the Father's words from Heaven, because your ministry really is your relationship with God. Jesus told me that His ministry was His relationship with the Father. If you want to be in the ministry, then you just let your relationship with God be public. Then, when you speak to others, the Spirit of the Lord will speak through you what is on the Father's heart. You will be speaking the very words of the Father.

IT'S TIME TO TAKE BACK OUR COUNTRY

These words that you speak from Heaven are going to have power on the Earth. Again, your relationship with God is your ministry on the Earth. So, let the Father do His will and His bidding through you.

I want to ask you to set yourself up by putting yourself in a place where you hear your Father and then speak those words.

"My sheep hear My voice, and I know them, and they follow Me." John 10:27

PRAYER

I pray for everyone that they would have ears to hear and that they would hear Your voice and that they would allow You to speak, Father, and that they would repeat those words in the throne room and bring them into this earthly realm.

Lord, I thank you, that You are giving the people boldness to speak the Father's words in Jesus' name.

IT'S TIME TO TAKE BACK OUR COUNTRY

What did the Holy Spirit reveal to you regarding this prayer point?

_____

_____

_____

_____

_____

_____

_____

_____

_____

_____

_____

_____

_____

_____

_____

_____

_____

_____

_____

_____

_____

_____

IT'S TIME TO TAKE BACK OUR COUNTRY

PRAYER POINT

9

Pray For Mercy

"Nevertheless in Your great mercy You did not utterly consume them nor forsake them; For You are God, gracious and merciful." (Nehemiah 9:31)

We are to pray for the enemies of God to be dealt with, but we also have to pray for mercy as well. One of the reasons that we have to pray for mercy is because there are people that are caught in the balance, and there are many people that don't even know what is going on around them.

There are nations that are already being judged. There are people that are not adhering to what God's plan is; they are not believers, and they are working against God. These people are already under a curse. They are already in judgment. Jesus said that we could ask for mercy. That is what Abraham did with Sodom and Gomorrah. Abraham actually delayed the judgment of Sodom and Gomorrah when it was supposed to happen right away.

"And the Lord said, "Because the outcry against Sodom and Gomorrah is great, and because their sin is very grave, I will go down now and see whether they have done altogether according to the outcry against it that has come to Me; and if not, I will know."

Then the men turned away from there and went toward Sodom, but Abraham still stood before the Lord. And Abraham came near and said, "Would You also destroy the righteous with the wicked? Suppose there were fifty righteous within the city; would You also destroy the place and not spare it for the fifty righteous that were in it? Far be it from You to do such a thing as this, to slay the righteous with the wicked, so that the righteous should be as the wicked; far be it from You! Shall not the Judge of all the Earth do right?"

So the Lord said, "If I find in Sodom fifty righteous within the city, then I will spare all the place for their sakes."

Then Abraham answered and said, "Indeed now, I who am but dust and ashes have taken it upon myself to speak to the Lord: Suppose there were five less than the fifty righteous; would You destroy all of the city for lack of five?"

IT'S TIME TO TAKE BACK OUR COUNTRY

So He said, "If I find there forty-five, I will not destroy it."

And he spoke to Him yet again and said, "Suppose there should be forty found there?"

So He said, "I will not do it for the sake of forty."

Then he said, "Let not the Lord be angry, and I will speak: Suppose thirty should be found there?"

So He said, "I will not do it if I find thirty there."

And he said, "Indeed now, I have taken it upon myself to speak to the Lord: Suppose twenty should be found there?"

So He said, "I will not destroy it for the sake of twenty."

Then he said, "Let not the Lord be angry, and I will speak but once more: Suppose ten should be found there?"

And He said, "I will not destroy it for the sake of ten." So the Lord went His way as soon as He had finished speaking with Abraham; and Abraham returned to his place."
Genesis 18:20-33

The judgment on Sodom and Gomorrah did happen, but it was delayed. There were some people that needed to be retrieved out of there, and that is where we are at right now. We pray for mercy, so people are retrieved and do not go to hell.

IT'S TIME TO TAKE BACK OUR COUNTRY

PRAYER

Father, we thank You in the name of Jesus that You will have mercy on our nation and that Father, You withhold any evil planned by the enemy. That You would extend Your mercy and that there would be a great move of Your Spirit on this Earth. Father, I thank You that there will be many that come into Your kingdom through salvation in the name of Jesus, amen

IT'S TIME TO TAKE BACK OUR COUNTRY

What did the Holy Spirit reveal to you regarding this prayer point?

_____

_____

_____

_____

_____

_____

_____

_____

_____

_____

_____

_____

_____

_____

_____

_____

_____

_____

_____

_____

_____

_____

_____

_____

IT'S TIME TO TAKE BACK OUR COUNTRY

PRAYER POINT

10

Cut Off The Plans Of The Enemy

"Finally, my brethren, be strong in the Lord and in the power of His might. Put on the whole armor of God, that you may be able to stand against the wiles of the devil. For we do not wrestle against flesh and blood, but against principalities, against powers, against the rulers of the darkness of this age, against spiritual hosts of wickedness in the heavenly places." (Ephesians 6:10-12)

Jesus showed me that the enemy has tried to infiltrate to the point that even our fundamental rights are taken away. The enemy is trying to confuse people about our rights as Americans in particular. As believers, we need to pray often because evil spirits are infiltrating people. When these evils spirits infiltrate people and begin manifesting, it causes people to question the

IT'S TIME TO TAKE BACK OUR COUNTRY

Constitution and our very history, which creates controversy. You can see this played out on an almost daily basis, especially in the United States. This is why we must pray daily that the plans of the enemy are cut off. We need to push back against the evil infiltration and let the glory of our Father be manifest.

PRAYER

Father, in the name of Jesus, we bind all evil spirits from trying to convince people to take away our rights as human beings and as Americans in this country.

We thank you, God, that you have given us the ability to exercise authority over evil spirits. We bind, and we push those evil spirits out and that our Constitution will stay intact.

And Father, that You will give us wisdom and revelation on how to deal with these evil spirits. We bind all of them now. We drive out evil spirits in the name of Jesus. And I thank You, Lord. We thank You for our freedom. We thank You for our freedom in Christ and for the nation that we live in as well. Amen

IT'S TIME TO TAKE BACK OUR COUNTRY

What did the Holy Spirit reveal to you regarding this prayer point?

_____

_____

_____

_____

_____

_____

_____

_____

_____

_____

_____

_____

_____

_____

_____

_____

_____

_____

_____

_____

_____

_____

_____

_____

_____

_____

IT'S TIME TO TAKE BACK OUR COUNTRY

PRAYER POINT

11

<u>The Justice System</u>

"Righteousness and justice are the foundation of Your throne; Mercy and truth go before Your face." (Psalm 89:14)

The Lord showed me clearly that we must pray for our justice system, and for the Attorney General. The Lord spoke with me at length about the Attorney General and that He wants us to target him in prayer. We have been praying for the Attorney General specifically since May 2020. Ever since our ministry has made it public that we need to pray for the Attorney General, we continually see how God is using him to clean house.

The justice system and the Attorney General has become a real focus for us because Jesus said that He has already taken care of our president. We must continue to pray for him, but God has already established his presidency.

During the visitation I had in May of 2020, the Lord showed me the Attorney General with a stack of indictments in his hand that must go through. When these people are indicted, it will set an example to others. When these indictments are handed out, it will put fear in people that are doing these terrible things, so this is something we need to pray for. We pray for the justice system and we pray for the Attorney General because he must be given the ability to push these indictments through without them being stopped in any way.

PRAYER

Father we pray for the Attorney General and I thank you, Lord, that that he has strength and power and that he feels the anointing and the yoke breaking power right now in the name of Jesus. We pray that You use him mightily to bring to justice those who will not repent of their wicked sins against children and the weak in the name of Jesus. I break the power of every evil spirit that is infiltrating people and causing them to commit criminal acts at the highest level.

IT'S TIME TO TAKE BACK OUR COUNTRY

What did the Holy Spirit reveal to you regarding this prayer point?

_____

_____

_____

_____

_____

_____

_____

_____

_____

_____

_____

_____

_____

_____

_____

_____

_____

_____

_____

_____

_____

_____

_____

_____

_____

_____

IT'S TIME TO TAKE BACK OUR COUNTRY

PRAYER POINT

12

The Five-Fold Ministry

"And He Himself gave some to be apostles, some prophets, some evangelists, and some pastors and teachers, for the equipping of the saints for the work of ministry, for the edifying of the body of Christ, till we all come to the unity of the faith and of the knowledge of the Son of God, to a perfect man, to the measure of the stature of the fullness of Christ; that we should no longer be children, tossed to and fro and carried about with every wind of doctrine, by the trickery of men, in the cunning craftiness of deceitful plotting, but, speaking the truth in love, may grow up in all things into Him who is the head—Christ— from whom the whole body, joined and knit together by what every joint supplies, according to the effective working by which every part does its share, causes growth

of the body for the edifying of itself in love." (Ephesians 4:11-16)

The Lord spoke at length with me about the faithful ministry of the church. The Lord has set in the church these five governments of God. These are the executive branches of God's government, the apostle, prophet, pastor, teacher, and evangelist. They are all set in the church to build up the body and to bring us into unity. When we have become mature saints, then the body is built up, and then we can go out and win the world for Jesus Christ.

The five-fold ministry is for the church to build us up, it is not to tear us down. The five-fold is not to prophesy doom to nations; it's to build up the nations. My prayer is that the five-fold ministry will prosper and that everyone will rise up and fulfill their part. This is what we need in this hour.

We need faithful ministries building up the body and not criticizing people. We don't need people causing division. We need people that will build up, according to what Paul said, into the maturity of the saints. This is what we are called to do.

PRAYER

Father, in the name of Jesus, I thank you for the faithful ministry of the church.

IT'S TIME TO TAKE BACK OUR COUNTRY

Every person is called to a part of the five-fold ministry of the church, and I pray that the power of the Holy Spirit comes upon you right now and that you are ignited with fire from the altar in the name of Jesus. Father, restore people back to the Lord. Restore their hope. Restore their calling. Bring clarity to their call. Lord, help people to know that they are not only called, but they are chosen as faithful ministers. If you are an apostle, prophet, pastor, teacher, or an evangelist, I pray that the fire God would be on you right now in the name of Jesus. Amen.

IT'S TIME TO TAKE BACK OUR COUNTRY

What did the Holy Spirit reveal to you regarding this prayer point?

_____

_____

_____

_____

_____

_____

_____

_____

_____

_____

_____

_____

_____

_____

_____

_____

_____

_____

_____

_____

_____

_____

_____

_____

PRAYER POINT

13

Pray In The Spirit

"But you, beloved, building yourselves up on your most holy faith, praying in the Holy Spirit, keep yourselves in the love of God, looking for the mercy of our Lord Jesus Christ unto eternal life." (Jude 20-21)

It is very crucial in this hour that we become so full of the Spirit and pray in tongues all the time. Praying in the Spirit builds you up in your most holy of faith, keeping you in the love of God. So, we all need that. There is no one that prays in tongues too much.

"I thank my God I speak with tongues more than you all;"
1 Corinthians 14:18

IT'S TIME TO TAKE BACK OUR COUNTRY

Paul did pray in tongues more times than anyone. So, you need to extend your time praying in tongues. The devil will fight you on this more than just about anything else. Sometimes you literally have to lock yourself in a room for ten minutes, refuse to look at your phone, refuse to answer your door, refuse to do anything during that ten minutes other than praying in tongues. And then from that ten minutes, you will begin to extend that time as you progress.

Of course, evil spirits will throw a fit because they cannot stop you if you isolate yourself. You have to do this at least ten minutes a day, pray in the spirit, and then pray to yourself. Learn how to pray to yourself in a whisper, in tongues, as often as you can. I used to pray thirteen hours a day at work because I could pray while I was working. I learned how to pray under my breath, and people didn't know what I was doing. However, when I would do this at work, the evil spirits got stirred up in people.

The evil spirits would speak to me through people saying, "What are you doing? What is that thing you're doing? I don't like that."

And I'm like, "What? Praying in the tongues?"

"Yeah. Don't do that!"

IT'S TIME TO TAKE BACK OUR COUNTRY

Those evil spirits knew what I was doing even though no one could hear me! So, we need to pray in tongues for an extended period of time, and then God will move in our lives and the lives of those around us.

PRAYER

Father anoint people right now. Let them sense Your Holy Spirit so strongly and let them begin praying and flowing in the fire of God. I thank You that your people are receiving the power of the Holy Spirit right now and that you are catching them up in the realm of the Spirit. Pray the mysteries of God right now. Build yourself up in your most holy faith, praying in the Holy Spirit. The Lord is making you strong by causing you to pray out the perfect will of God.

According to Romans 8:26, the Spirit Himself is making intercession for us with groanings which cannot be uttered. Every one of us is going to pray in tongues. We are going to pray out the mysteries. We are not going to be bashful about it. We are going to be bold in the name of Jesus. And I thank you, Lord God, for a special anointing and impartation right now that everyone everywhere will pray in the spirit. Yes, in Jesus' name. Hallelujah!

*If you do not yet pray in tongues, the gift of praying in tongues is for all those who believe in Jesus. When you are able to find a time to get alone and pray, ask the Lord to fill you with the Holy Spirit with the evidence of speaking in tongues. It will come from your spirit and not your mind. In other words, it will just flow out of you. The important thing is that you simply open up your mouth and begin to speak what is coming up from within. When we ask, we receive. We just have to ask like a little child!

IT'S TIME TO TAKE BACK OUR COUNTRY

What did the Holy Spirit reveal to you regarding this prayer point?

_____

_____

_____

_____

_____

_____

_____

_____

_____

_____

_____

_____

_____

_____

_____

_____

_____

_____

_____

_____

_____

_____

_____

_____

IT'S TIME TO TAKE BACK OUR COUNTRY

PRAYER POINT

14

Take A Stand For Righteousness

"Then the righteous will answer Him, saying, 'Lord, when did we see You hungry and feed You, or thirsty and give You drink? When did we see You a stranger and take You in, or naked and clothe You? Or when did we see You sick, or in prison, and come to You?' And the King will answer and say to them, 'Assuredly, I say to you, inasmuch as you did it to one of the least of these My brethren, you did it to Me.'" (Matthew 25:37-40)

Every Christian needs to take a stand for righteousness. When you take a stand for righteousness, then you become the standard for your area. Whether it's at your church, on your job, or within your own home, people will know you by the choices you make. For instance, if you choose not to speak bad about someone but instead choose to speak good of someone, you are taking a stand for righteousness. If you choose to do good instead of something bad, you are taking a stand for righteousness. If you choose to side with children and vote for children and give children a voice, you are taking a stand for righteousness.

"Pure and undefiled religion before God and the Father is this: to visit orphans and widows in their trouble, and to keep oneself unspotted from the world." James 1:27

To take a stand for righteousness, we are going to fight for the fatherless and the widow. We are going to pay their rent and help them. We are going to love on them. We are going to give to children who don't have much. We are going to give to single mothers. We are going to give to people that can't give back. To take a stand for righteousness is to do these acts of righteousness. Not for the applause of man, but we do all these things as unto the Lord.

"'Take heed that you do not do your charitable deeds before men, to be seen by them. Otherwise you have no reward from your Father in heaven. Therefore, when you do a charitable deed, do not sound a trumpet before you as the hypocrites do in the synagogues and in the streets, that they may have glory from men. Assuredly, I say to you, they have their reward. But when you do a charitable deed, do not let your left hand know what your right hand is doing, that your charitable deed may be in secret; and your

IT'S TIME TO TAKE BACK OUR COUNTRY

Father who sees in secret will Himself reward you openly."'
Matthew 6:1-4

You can do things for people, and that will speak louder than words. Do things to help people that cannot help themselves. Start today; listen for who the Holy Spirit wants you to target, to take a stand for righteousness. It could be as simple as buying someone a can of beans, whatever you can do, give to someone else. Sow into someone else's life and help people out and tell them that God loves them.

If you are willing to take a stand for righteousness, God will put people in your path who will have a need that you can help with. They may need a blanket, socks, food, etc. There are all kinds of things you can do for a very good price. We can all do this. You can buy somebody a pair of socks. Pray and ask the Lord who you can give to. These are all acts of righteousness, and you can pray that God gives you strategies.

PRAYER

Father, give us a "God idea" about what we can do for people. Show us how we can minister to our neighbors. Show us how we can minister to people without even using words. Give us compassion and the ability to do things for others who can't even pay us back. Father, I thank You for giving us the provision, even if it's just a dollar, so that we can buy a pair of socks for someone in need. We thank you

IT'S TIME TO TAKE BACK OUR COUNTRY

that you will provide for us so we can provide for others in Jesus' name. Amen.

IT'S TIME TO TAKE BACK OUR COUNTRY

What did the Holy Spirit reveal to you regarding this prayer point?

_____

_____

_____

_____

_____

_____

_____

_____

_____

_____

_____

_____

_____

_____

_____

_____

_____

_____

_____

_____

_____

_____

_____

_____

_____

IT'S TIME TO TAKE BACK OUR COUNTRY

PRAYER POINT

15

The Goodness Of God

"Now the Lord descended in the cloud and stood with him there and proclaimed the name of the Lord. And the Lord passed before him and proclaimed, "The Lord, the Lord God, merciful and gracious, longsuffering, and abounding in goodness and truth" (Exodus 34:5-6)

You will find this out when you get to Heaven, and it shouldn't be a surprise for the body of Christ, but it seems to be a news flash that *God is a good God*. It's amazing how people get offended when you start telling them that God's not doing all these terrible things that are happening around the world. God is not judging people this way; the devil is the one that is doing these things. The devil is the god of this world. God, our Father, is not in charge of this world. It wouldn't be in a mess if

IT'S TIME TO TAKE BACK OUR COUNTRY

He was. So please don't insult my Father by saying that He is doing terrible things to people. When people at work would use the Lord's name in vain, I would tell them not to insult my Father. I would tell them that He is all I've got and explain that He is my Savior. When people would use the Lord's name in vain at work, I would say, "Yes, let Him be praised. Let's worship Him. He is worthy. He is good." And then they just wouldn't know what to say.

So many people have had a rough life, and I can certainly understand that. People have gone through so much trauma because of all the things that have happened to them. It's a broken world, but it's not God's fault. We need to proclaim Him as good, and we need to tell other people that God is being slandered. It's not God doing these terrible things. God doesn't have sickness to give anyone. There is no sickness or trauma in Heaven. There is no storehouse of sickness, pain, or torment in Heaven.

"how God anointed Jesus of Nazareth with the Holy Spirit and with power, who went about doing good and healing all who were oppressed by the devil, for God was with Him." Acts 10:38

Jesus went around healing everyone who was oppressed of the devil. He was doing good and healing everyone everywhere. The Father, Son, and Holy Spirit only want to do good for people. We have to understand this once and for all. Despite all that people have been through, He is a good Father. Let's believe that people's perceptions in this area will begin to shift.

PRAYER

Father, in the name of Jesus, we pray that believers everywhere will have this shift in their personality, in their perception that they see You as a good God, and then they go out and give the good news of a good God to the people. That they would go out and proclaim Your goodness and that people's sins have been paid for and that they just need to repent and accept Jesus. I thank You, Father, that You will give all the people reading this, the boldness to proclaim Your goodness in the name of Jesus.

IT'S TIME TO TAKE BACK OUR COUNTRY

What did the Holy Spirit reveal to you regarding this prayer point?

_____

_____

_____

_____

_____

_____

_____

_____

_____

_____

_____

_____

_____

_____

_____

_____

_____

_____

_____

_____

_____

_____

_____

_____

_____

PRAYER POINT

16

Can God Count On You?

"And whatever you do, do it heartily, as to the Lord and not to men, knowing that from the Lord you will receive the reward of the inheritance; for you serve the Lord Christ." (Colossians 3:23-24)

Jesus Himself gave me all these prayer points so that we would have a strategic direction to pray in and believe for change in our families and the nation in which we live.

I ask that you read these prayer points over and over again so we can see swift changes and immediate answers to these prayers. I am counting on you to come into unity with everyone else that is reading these same prayers. When we do this, it is going to change history!

IT'S TIME TO TAKE BACK OUR COUNTRY

Right now, this is our prayer assignment to push back the darkness. Thank you all for praying with me. Thank you from the Father's heart, who is saying thank you for standing up for righteousness and taking your nation back.

You take care of things in the Spirit first, and then go to the polls, and vote. You must also go to your neighbor and represent God in the right way and tell them that He is a good God.

I feel that what is going to happen is that there will be so much revealed through people's mouths in government that they are going to disqualify themselves. That is what I am seeing in the Spirit.

So, pray, pray, pray, pray, pray!

Let's force the enemy to just go ahead and reveal all of his schemes and strategies and embarrass himself. It's getting to the place where I don't think the devil would even vote for himself! The enemy is so confused right now that I don't even think he knows what he believes anymore because it's pretty clear that there's a lot of confusion in the enemy's camp, which is really what we want. We *want* confusion in the enemy's camp. We saw this same thing happen in the Old Testament:

IT'S TIME TO TAKE BACK OUR COUNTRY

"'I will send My fear before you, I will cause confusion among all the people to whom you come, and will make all your enemies turn their backs to you.'" Exodus 23:27

The enemies of God would turn on themselves, and the people of God would sit and watch the armies fight themselves and kill each other. That is what I see happening in the very near future.

When the time comes, vote for the life of the children in the womb. Jesus told me that from now on, every child that is born is a prophet. So, we have to protect these children. We are going to vote for righteousness and justice in our system. We are going to vote to have our country back because it really is the people's country. It's not the government's; it's the people's country. We hired the government to work for us.

The government works for us. The government enforces and protects us, it does not tell us what we believe. They do not tell us what we can and can't do with our faith. The enemy has crossed the line, so now the people are going to rise up!

Let's stay watchful and in prayer and keep giving the devil a headache every day!

IT'S TIME TO TAKE BACK OUR COUNTRY

PRAYER

Father, I thank You for every single person that has read this book and committed to pray for these specific areas. I pray for every area of their lives and am believing that you are going to bless them and restore everything back to them seven-fold for what the enemy has stolen.

I pray that you raise up mighty men, women, and children in these days to do the greater works and to live holy, passionate lives for you, Jesus. Amen!

IT'S TIME TO TAKE BACK OUR COUNTRY

What did the Holy Spirit reveal to you regarding this final section?

_____
_____
_____
_____
_____
_____
_____
_____
_____
_____
_____
_____
_____
_____
_____
_____
_____
_____
_____
_____
_____
_____
_____
_____
_____

OTHER BOOKS BY KEVIN L. ZADAI

You Can Hear God's Voice

Receiving from Heaven

It's Rigged in Your Favor

*Praying from the Heavenly Realms Heavenly
Visitation*

Supernatural Finances

The Agenda of Angels

The Mystery of the Power Words

IT'S TIME TO TAKE BACK OUR COUNTRY

Join our network at **Warriornotes.tv**.
Join our ministry and training school at **Warrior Notes School of Ministry**.

Visit **KevinZadai.com** for more info.

IT'S TIME TO TAKE BACK OUR COUNTRY

Made in the USA
Monee, IL
28 November 2020

49825934R00049